CASS

BUTCHER

BUNTING

First published by Edward Arnold (Australia) Pty Ltd 1977, ISBN 0726709999
Monash University New Plays no 1: general editor Mary Lord.

This re-issue published by Reed Independent, Dandenong, Australia, 2015.

Winner of the Alexander Theatre Playwriting Competition 1976.

Printed by Createspace.com, a division of Amazon.com.

Cover illustration: 'almost there', uploader Kalebp, Google Openclipart

Available from Amazon.com, Createspace.com and all leading bookshops and
outlets with online ordering facilities. Ebook available from all leading e-stores.

National Library of Australia Cataloguing-in-Publication entry
Creator: Reed, Bill, 1939- author.
Title: Cass Butcher Bunting / Bill Reed.ISBN: 9780994322722 (paperback)
Subjects: Australian drama --20th century.
Dewey Number: A822.3

National Library of Australia Cataloguing-in-Publication entry
Creator: Reed, Bill, 1939- author.
Title: Cass Butcher Bunting / Bill Reed
ISBN: 9780994322739 (ebook)
Subjects: Australian drama --20th century.
Dewey Number: A822.3

CASS BUTCHER BUNTING

a play by

BILL REED

R

Works by Bill Reed
The Pipwink Papers\
Me, the Old Man
Stigmata
Ihe
Dogod
Crooks
Tusk
Throw her back
Are You Human?
Tasker Tusker Tasker
Awash
1001 Lankan Nights book 1
1001 Lankan Nights book 2
Water Workout (Nonfiction)

plays
Burke's Company
Truganinni
The Pecking Order
Mr Siggie Morrison with his Comb and Paper*
Jack Charles is Up and Fighting
Just Out of Your Ground
You Want It, Don't You, Billy?
I Don't Know What to Do with You!
Paddlesteamer
Cass Butcher Bunting
More Bullsh
Talking to a Mirror
Auntie and the Girl

award-winning short stories (see title 'Passing Strange')
Messman on the C.E. Altar
English Expression
The 200-year Old Feet
The Case Inside
Blind Freddie Among the Pickle Jars
The Old Ex-serviceman
Mahood on the Thin Beach
The Shades of You my Dandenong

To a brave cast and director, and to Mary Lord.

INTRODUCTION

The resurgence of interest in Australia drama during the latter years of the last century produced a crop of young dramatists who enjoyed considerable success in their depictions of contemporary manners and mores, sometimes treated seriously, but most often seen from a mildly satirical viewpoint.

Bill Reed's 'Cass Butcher Bunting' is wholly serious but it is only contemporary in so far as it deals specifically with characters of the post-war – and now international-terror-driven -- generation. They and their dilemma could be transferred to any time and place without loss and the overriding theme of the play, the fear of being trapped in a situation of imminent destruction, is basic to all living creatures. The play is brutal and shocking and it is unremitting in the demands it makes of its audience. That it is far removed from the popular idea of 'entertainment' goes without saying. Its importance as a contribution to Australian dramatic writing is quite another matter.

The play begins with an explosion and a cave in down a mine shaft. Three miners are trapped there; Cass, the local golden boy, sometime star football player and medical student, now an ordinary worker in the mine, drug dependent and complete cynic; Butcher, the average product of a small mining town, inarticulate, unimaginative, who thinks that the best life can offer is a new motor car; and Bunting, an old-time miner with the typical miners' 'hump', lonely and taciturn with an obsession about the welfare of cats. The play explores the reactions of these three men to the disaster that has befallen them and the fate which awaits them.

Both Bunting and Cass have been injured by the explosion while Butcher suffers nothing more serious than shock. Cass's pain does not seem to result from the effects of the cave-in as much as from the apparent loss of his drugs for which he searches between severe bouts of withdrawal symptoms that become more painful as the play proceeds. Bunting's injuries are critical and he dies during the course of the play. He never regains full consciousness but moves intermittently between a near-catatonic state of total

1

incomprehension and delirium, during which he shouts barely decipherable ravings about cats being mutilated or destroyed in a variety of extremely sadistic ways. Bunting's words bear no relationship to the continuing dialogue between Cass and Butcher; they function as disturbing, almost surrealistic interjections of the single theme of human brutality to cats, a specific example of man's inhumanity to animals – but probably more so as a metaphor for the happenstance violence-in-disaster visited up the three men and, of course, upon their lost miner mates.

Man's fundamental inhumanity to man is a major theme explored in 'Cass Butcher Bunting'. Bunting's ravings are reminders that in the modern world this inhumanity is most often expressed in cruelty to animals. The exchanges between Cass and Butcher and their varying reactions to each other can be seen as subtle revelations of aspects of this theme which Bill Reed has explored in a situation as near to the extreme as can be imagined.

The setting of the action deep in the bowels of the earth places so-called civilised man back in a primordial situation, in a closed-off cave, his only weapons rocks and stones, his battle against impending death, his companions two work-mates. Butcher, the ordinary man (average man? Everyman?) responds to the explosion with shock, rising panic and then optimistic practicality – he tries to make contact with the world outside by persistently tapping on a pipe which runs through the mine. Inarticulate and unintelligent as he (intelligently!) thinks he is, he looks to Cass for explanations and support. They grew up together, went to school together until Butcher, like his father before him, went to work in the mine and Cass, unlike his father, went on to scholastic and sporting triumphs. He then became Butcher's personal hero and the proud boast of the township.

Cass, on the other hand, having found himself to be undistinguished, if not an abject failure, despite all the promise he had before him... and having grown past the township's narrow horizons through his sheer excelling abilities... is trapped at a time when he metaphorically has his tail between his legs. He and Butcher are now work mates and it made clear early on that Cass automatically takes command and stills his own fears in an attempt to help Butcher gain control of his rising terror. His repeated requests to Butcher to cool it have some effect. But this is only temporary; Butcher's agitation would be soothed by Cass's admonitions were it not for Bunting's unpredictable bursts of raving and contagious panic.

It becomes clear that, underneath their lifelong relationship there has existed a genuine and deep-seated incompatibility. Cass's highly-cultivated imagination – revolving around his own inflated image of himself – gave him such an exaggerated idea of his own abilities that he eventually failed when he faced the competition of the larger world and retreated into drugs. After the disaster they find themselves barely surviving, he comes finally to see how death is to be accepted, if not actually wished for. He pierces the façade which makes the work-a-day world bearable and acknowledges his dislike for a mate who, he finds himself really believing, is dull-witted, unambitious and damned by his inability to change:

> CASS: Butcher, you've always been without poetry. It's... not only that I never liked you, Butcher; it's just that I don't want to die with you. Just don't come near me'.

Then there is Butcher's grievance which is also released and cannot any longer be held back:

> BUTCHER: You took away the only female I ever wanted, bastard. You hitched her up and then, bastard you, you ditched the only woman I ever wanted, and I vowed I was going to get you one day. Bastard.

Their imagined terrors are exacerbated when the dying Bunting begins to inhale and exhale deeply and loudly, to almost theatrical proportions as though he was burlesquing respiration. Butcher goes berserk and tries to batter the senseless Bunting into silence without regard for the consequences, but his efforts are entirely ineffectual. It is important to notice here, in the light of later events, that Butcher's violent attack on Bunting is not an act of malice but an act of terror. He believes Bunting is using up far more than his share of what little air remains and he is overwhelmed by the imminent fear of death by suffocation.

Cass's injuries from the first rock fall and the increasing intensity of his withdrawal pains have made it virtually impossible for him

3

to speak. However, after Butcher has for a time become the sole focus of attention for the audience, Cass lapses into a 'trip' and hallucinates, moving the play into a whole new dimension as the audience experiences Cass's mental state with him. During this section, Cass mixes reality with fantasy in nightmare proportions; there is, predictably, no logic to the action, no anchor for an audience to attach itself to.

One thing is clear: Cass or Bunting succeed in killing Bunting during one blackout by bashing his head in with a large rock. This puzzle is never resolved with any certainty in the text and so adds a special piquancy to the dialogue in the closing scenes.

After his 'trip' Cass enters a halcyon, painless period but has lost his power to dominate Butcher. Their verbal sparring, always potentially dangerous, is now reduced to the physical level as they arm themselves with rocks to keep each other at bay. Until this point their exchanges of mutual abuse have been stilled before they reach the stage of physical assault by ominous signs that the first explosion will not the last. Rock falls, small provocative needling have become more or less diversions to pass the time.

Bunting's death provides a new diversion. Their 'requiem' for him is as dramatically unconventional and as convincingly realistic as the rest of the play. It shows two fellow workers paying their last respects to a third by giving a cool and sardonic account of him. There is none of the heart-rending veneer of sentimentality so beloved of our early balladeers and fiction writers, none of the platitudes essential to the funeral as a social occasion.

The 'requiem' for Bunting during which Cass and Butcher were in agreement and were, moreover, united in mood and attitude has shown that, in spite of their obvious and apparently irreconcilable differences, they have something indefinable in common. In an unconscious desire to strengthen this bond each is moved to justify himself and his life to the other, to explain his successes and failures. In a way, each offer a requiem for himself. This leads to an unspoken but real understanding, forgiveness and acceptance. When they hear the approach of the final catastrophe and recognise it for what it is, they move together and, in a final gesture which boasts of their proud membership in the brotherhood of man, wave their penises in defiance of death. Thus they die brandishing the ultimate symbol of the life force, ironic as it may be under these circumstances.

The complexities of 'Cass Butcher Bunting' do not immediately reveal themselves and, in any case are by no means contained in the dialogue; at least a third of the text is taken up by what are technically known as stage directions, but here these are equally important to understanding as the dialogue. In performance, sound, light and action share equal importance with the spoken word. This divergence from orthodoxy is an essential ingredient in a drama which shows, among other things, that inescapable inarticulateness and natural reticence, along with pride that is undeniable, are major barriers to mutual understanding even among those who have as much in common as Cass and Butcher.

This point is reflected in the dialogue itself which is repetitious and thin, intended as it is, to express feelings rather than ideas and to show that language can often be a very real barrier to communication. Bunting's sporadic outbursts do not advance the action, are rarely complete sentences, but do in general show man's need for warmth and companionship. Butcher who speaks most of the dialogue is more a man of action than of words and has a very limited vocabulary which consists largely of expletives and obscenities. Try as he might his attempts at communications are usually vague and groping; he is the victim of limitations of which he is unaware. Cass, although highly intelligent, is hampered by pain and his own drug-withdrawn escape into a world of fantasy he finds inexpressible.

Although 'Cass Butcher Bunting' is a full-length play it does not observe the usual conventions of act divisions; rather it is divided into 26 sections of varying length, most of which are indicated by blackouts. The play could run continuously or could be broken by an interval or intervals. In the original production at the Alexander Theatre the play ran continuously without the section endings being indicated and a normal interval at the end of section 11 gave the impression of a play in two acts. This fluidity in the overall dramatic structure reflects the relative unconventionality of the play.

The play works, as suggested earlier, on a number of levels. It may be seen simply as a straightforward drama about a disaster in a mine shaft or, as one reviewer claimed, 'a powerful expose of a restricted mining community which is as claustrophobic and as destructive as any rock tomb'. It may, as the playwright replied to a newspaper interviewer, be 'about *dying* not death'.

Unarguably it is in the face of impending and inevitable death that man, with nothing more to lose, can step out from behind his everyday mask and reveal his needs and his weaknesses, acknowledge and accept his failures. Between the simple social comment suggested by the reviewer and the distinction of 'getting through' more than the acceptance of death put forward by the playwright, lie a number of layers of meaning which the individual member of the audience or the reader will find for himself.

Mary Lord
General Editor
Monash New Plays series
Monash University, Melbourne

CASS BUTCHER BUNTING

THE PREMIERE

Winner of the Alexander Theatre Playwriting Competition 1976, CASS BUTCHER BUNTING was first performed by the Alexander Theatre Company of Monash University on June 16 1976 with the following cast:

Cass   Hamish Hughes
Butcher   Burt Cooper
Bunting   Tom Lake
Production design and directed by Peter Williams
Lighting and special effects by Bill Akers
Set design by Graeme McGuffie

THE PLAY

1.

The stage is dark. There is an atmosphere of damp dust, of unhealthy and depressing depth.

Sound grows slowly, just as heavy work on stage becomes more and more perceptible through the darkness. The sound somehow encapsulates the very internal crashing insistence of technology.

Two or three 'lighting flashes' allow the set to be assessed. What the audience can discern is a coal face in one of the deep crosscuts of the pit. The three men working there are doing so evidently in an unusual part of the mine since they are cramped so uncomfortably. It is as if they want to get the work there over with quickly so that can get out of that 'pocket' they've been assigned to work in.

Rather than diminish, the sound of the mine increases to a crescendo until a sudden contrasting silence. Then shouting from far away. Then a shock wave of a deep explosion pushes upwards and through. Then the sound of the rock falling in everywhere and the shaft caving in.

The cave-in fills the whole theatre, continues, then stops abruptly. Silence. Then there is nearby moaning before a renewed silence that quickly become claustrophobic.

The stage is now pitch black. A long pause before a scream breaks through, replaced then by what sounds like a monotonal raving, low and incoherent. It is coming from BUNTING.

Thin and even-disorientating lighting allows the audience to pick out and follow the men, even though they themselves remain in a terrifying total darkness. The audience sees that BUTCHER is the liviest, at this stage, of the three. He is groping around... but only really near himself and obviously in too much shock to do much else as yet. Any purchase he can make on the rock around him he clings on to for a moment as though it could be a life saver.

BUNTING is sitting up against the rock face away from BUTCHER. He can be seen and heard to be in an incoherent but transfixed state.

CASS is stretched out flat, almost as if he had been neatly laid out there. He is so still he could be unconscious, for any who cannot see the wild rolling of his eyes.

Suddenly BUTCHER screams again; this time it is more forceful than the outcry that came through the pitch blackness earlier; this time it is more measured, more an expression of anger.

CASS rolls his eyes over to BUTCHER's direction and:)

CASS (strangely languid) Yes?

BUTCHER *Who?*

CASS Cass.

BUTCHER *Where?!*

(Butcher tries to grope towards Cass. It proves an unsuccessful attempt. Cass does not help him by talking so as

the other man can be guided to where he is; nor is Butcher keen to 'launch' himself out into the pitch blackness. Butcher gives up the attempt, begins to shake)

BUTCHER   Fucking hell, Cass.

CASS   Yep.

BUTCHER   *Jesus.*

CASS   Yeah.

BUTCHER   You alright?

CASS   You alright?

BUTCHER   Chrissakes, Cass.

CASS   I know.

BUTCHER   *Where are you?*

CASS   (sotto voce) In my tomb.

BUTCHER   What?

CASS   (harder) In my tomb, Butcher.

BUTCHER   Jesus.

CASS   Stay still.

BUTCHER (not comprehending) What?

CASS Still. Stay still.

BUTCHER What?

CASS Jesus. Stay still!

> *(Silence, while Butcher tries very hard to suppress his mounting hysteria. It is all he can do to keep himself from crying out again. Cass, even though he is just as fearful, forces himself to lie back again)*

CASS (crooningly) Stay still stay still stay still. Stay still, Butcher.

> *(This has a calming influence on them both. Butcher manages to calm himself such that only his breathing comes through shallow and irregular. Relative silence, which makes Bunting's outburst all the more alarming)*

BUNTING Cats! Catscatscatscats….!

> *(He drops suddenly to mumbling. Both Cass and Butcher have frozen with alarm)*

BUTCHER What was that?
>   (no answer)
Who's *there*?
>   (gets no reply)
Bunting? You alright, Bunting?

(He forces himself to crawl towards where he thinks Bunting must be, guided by the latter's mumbling)

BUTCHER   Bunting.

BUNTING   (suddenly)   Cats barbed tried writhing wired barbarous barbed wiredaround. Yes.

BUTCHER (overcoming fright) Cass, it's Bunting.

CASS   Yes.

BUTCHER   He's sitting up like a zombie.

CASS   Keep it level, Butcher.

BUTCHER What's going on?

CASS Absorb it, Butcher.

BUTCHER   Fuck that.

CASS Get to know it.

BUTCHER   FUCK THAT!

(Pause. But Butcher's agitation only increases because of it; he can't withstand it any longer)

BUTCHER   I wanna know what happened. I wanna talk about it. *Cass.*

CASS Stay still first. For a bit.

BUTCHER You hurt?

CASS Don't, Butcher.

BUTCHER *Cass*!

CASS (explodes) Look…!
     (checks himself)
Still, stay still, see.

BUTCHER What're you on about?

CASS It's happened, see.

BUTCHER I know it's bloody happened, Cass.

CASS No, it's happened, Butcher.

BUTCHER Christ, man, what's bloody happened?!

CASS (calmly into air) Haven't you always known it was going
to happen, Butcher?

BUTCHER *What*?

2.

BUNTING (lyrical burst) Cats set alight in the phone box the
kero tin left charred alongside of. Cat gut spasm on the poison
laid. Yes.

BUTCHER   (spooked) Jesus, what's he saying?

(gets no answer back from Cass who is holding himself 'in' for all his might. In the heavy silence Butcher tries to crawl over to Cass, but he cannot locate him, even though he misses him only narrowly. Cass does not help, nor, again, is Butcher too keen on doing too much groping around blindly)

BUTCHER   Cass, I'm trying to find you. Say something. Where are you, Cass?

(He stops to listen for Cass's breathing, but Cass deliberately holds his breath in a hunch about what Butcher is trying to do)

BUTCHER   Cass, you breathing?
(no reply)
Don't leave a man alone, Cass. *Cass.* CASS!

(Butcher's hysteria is visibly rising again. It bursts out when he traces the rock stratum to find out how low it is over his head. He only just manages to stifle another scream for help.

Bunting joins in as though joining in singing.   His babble takes over. Butcher tries to move towards him to stop him, but cannot and can only cover his ears.

Bunting stops his maddenng screeching suddenly.)

CASS   Cool, Butcher, cool.   Roll your mind around it.   Try consuming.

BUNTING (again frightfully) Cats of kittens of cats drowned they were. Inrush a lungful, why dontcha? Come halfdrowned in the sea of waves. Wave to the kitty, dontcha? Cats swimming by the side of the ship trying to crawl up a steel side. Hull it's called and them cats did I see. Yes.

(stops just as suddenly. Pause)

CASS Alive, Butcher. Simple.

BUTCHER You call this alive, Cass? Cass?

CASS Not so simple. Not so simple, is it, Butcher?

BUTCHER Listen, Cass, mate….

CASS Alive, Butcher. Still in the here's-me.

BUTCHER Cass, you've got to listen to me.

CASS (simply) No.

BUTCHER Chrissakes, Cass, where are you?
    (no reply)
It's not much to ask, Cass. Just let me touch you. Cass…

BUNTING (burst again) Half cat half nothing. Nothing half of nothing. Left, dontcha know. Like it was sawn in two. Yes. There in front of me around the back down by the side lane by the club rooms there. Its two back legs and half a body is all thatssall. Oh. Yes.

BUTCHER SHUT YOUR ARSE!

16

(He swings a back-hand swipe in Bunting's direction this goes nowhere near the other man. Controls himself before turning to CASS's direction)

BUTCHER   You think I'm weak as piss, Cass.

(Cass is seen to open his eyes suddenly, as though he has just seen how low the rock formation is hanging over his head. He reaches up repugnantly just as Butcher had and is better able to relatively calmly trace the surface with the back of his hand. 'then he too panics and is barely able to control himself before he cries out.   It comes as a gurgle)

BUTCHER   (listening hard) Cass...?

(Cass finally manages a strangely croaked and bitter laugh. This makes Butcher angry)

BUTCHER   You reckon I'm as weak as piss.   Who're you, Cass?
   (then weakly)
Chrissakes, all I want to do is feel you.

CASS   Bunting.

BUTCHER   Bunting?
   (turns to Bunting's direction)
Bunting... all right now?

(He gropes his way over and this time manages to find Bunting.   He traces the old man's face with his fingers; Bunting neither moves or changes his expression as Butcher probes what he can now discern as a large gash on Bunting's head)

17

BUTCHER Blood, Cass. It's gotta be blood.

CASS Sure.

BUTCHER I think he's hurt bad.

CASS Shit, man, it's showing clearly. We can't see it showing clearly, Butcher.

(Butcher shakes Bunting hard. At least it gets Bunting to turn his head towards Butcher, but his expression can be seen to be unchanged)

BUNTING Yes. And in the market, cats. Stalling kittens. Day old, yes. A dollar going. Buy the kid a… and at the end of the day did I see him fling it into the furnace out back. A giggle it was.

BUTCHER (strained) He's not going to be any help, Cass.

CASS A help? Bunting? (snorts) You'd be lucky.

BUTCHER Let me touch you, Cass.

CASS Still. Stay still's better, Butcher.

BUTCHER I ain't that big time, Cass.

CASS No.

BUTCHER (outcry) JEEE-SUS!

CASS (ditto) YES!

(Pause. They both have to control themselves again)

BUTCHER I have to talk about it, Cass.

CASS Yes.

BUTCHER *What happened*?

CASS Your lamp work, Butcher?

BUTCHER (bemused) Must've lost my cap. Yours?

CASS Must've been the way I fell. Here's a question, Butcher…
could I have fallen any other way if I'd tried?
        (no reply)
Bunting's?

*(Butcher grunts the logic of that, gets back to Bunting and
groves around for his helmet. He can't find it)*

BUTCHER Can't find it, Cass.

CASS (amused) Ask him.

BUTCHER (seriously) He wouldn't know.

CASS (laugh) That right?

19

BUNTING (burst) Ears cut off the tabby. Wasn't it howling and and. Yes. I went to it but it died. But dead. Oh, yes.

BUTCHER He's giving me the shits, Cass.

CASS Give it slack, Butcher.

BUTCHER You can talk. What areya, subhuman?

CASS Subbed.

BUTCHER You tell me what happened.

CASS Is there a hurry? No hurry.

BUTCHER Fuck that, Cass.

CASS I want to hurry, mate. No hurry. We hurry we die quicker. Butcher, just shrug and live now.

BUTCHER Up yours too.

CASS We hurry, we go down screaming, Butcher.

BUTCHER Don't talk to me like an idiot.
    (thinks on that, then angrily)
Don't talk to me like a fucking child, shithead.

CASS We hurry, we...

    (stops, losing control almost)

BUTCHER (premonition) *Jesus.*

CASS (gagging) We hurry it, Butcher... subhumaned... animals... asking a no god, yeah... for everything, Butcher. Mind leavings... dro... dross, Butcher.

BUTCHER (stopping up his mouth) Uh.

CASS It's always been com... coming, Butcher. It was...

(Butcher can't hold his gagging any more. As soon as he starts up, Cass's panic likewise wells up. He literally joins in outcry with Butcher and their outcries threaten to turn into full on screams until they exhaust themselves. They sound like two animals in the abattoirs.

As they slowly get themselves under control again, they enter a new stage of how the situation is what it is and how it is inescapable for the time being.

Cass regains his senses first and half sits up with great difficulty, but then has to lie back in pain.

All this time, unheard but now heard, Bunting has been mumbling away and now bursts out again:)

BUNTING The greyhounds were given stolen cats. Practice runs did I see. Cat claws pulled out so no hurting the doggies. Grey and killing they were. Yes. And wire meshing tied around the cat's body and it, yes, tied that time to the mechanical hare. Ha ha what a giggle, eh. The greyhounds, they tear a lot and doesn't that cat not stop twitching. Twitching. You seen twitching? And you see that little girl one time wrench right off part of the head of that kitten? I did. Clap, clap. Yes.

21

(He fades back to mumbling. Butcher stays with the side of his face against the rock wall. Cass suddenly remembers something and gropes for his pocket. It has been ripped off. He heaves himself up as best he can and gropes around for whatever he was after from his pocket. He has no success)

BUTCHER   What're you doing?

CASS   Looking.

BUTCHER   Cut it out. It's getting on my nerves.

CASS   Get stuffed.

BUTCHER   (sotto voce)   All I say was the flash, Cass.

CASS   There was a flash alright.

BUTCHER   You hear them talk about it, but…

CASS   I don't want to hear that shit, Butcher.

BUTCHER   Big man.

CASS   Yeah.

BUTCHER   Always the champion.

CASS   If you say so, Butcher.

BUNTING (reburst) That cat, oh yes. That cat was crucified on a fruit box. Nails for its front paws and one both back ones and that cat's blood on the footpath. Blood bath blood path. Did I see.

BUTCHER We've got to shut him up, Cass.
    (Cass doesn't answer)
We never got any warning.

CASS Matter?

BUTCHER It matters, Cass. To me it matters.

CASS We're alive.

BUTCHER That's why it matters!

CASS (thinks about it, then) I'll pay that.

BUTCHER How long, Cass?
    (no reply)
Come on, how long we've been down here?

CASS Too long, what dyou think.

BUTCHER Listen, Cass.

CASS Too wide and long. All the colours going. It's been too long, okay, okay. Maybe I should've rolled down the schoolyard and tumbled straight on down into here. Y'reckon that would've been quicker and cleaner, Butcher?

BUTCHER All I'm talking about is I don't want to die, Cass.

23

CASS You'll die.

BUTCHER *Not like this!*

(Blackout)

3.

(During the black out, the audience feels the essential claustrophobia that the three men are experiencing. Bunting's mumbling takes of a new dimension of a whispering paranoia that Butcher in particular has been reacting to. Through this, each one's breathing, every little movement they make becomes heightened and magnified... sounding boards)

CASS Butcher, don't you find it strange... that you can't see a thing... yet you've got to fight to close your eyes?   Jesus, Butcher, it's a cruel threat, isn't it? A kilometre of it up there.

BUTCHER Cut it out.

BUNTING (almost normally) In the arsehole of the cat, yes, pieces of glass still out. Jags. Didn't it jag ya? And nice kids normally, they were sticking their tongues out at me. Here kitty-kitty, here.

BUTCHER Old dope.

CASS Even the vestiges of colours, go. You noticed, Butcher? No colours and you can hear yourself all the more. How grey, like, you are. But your... *thing...* keeps factorying on. Here we are here, earthed. No living function at all anymore, Butcher, and we're still churning it all on. How's that for ho bloody hum?

(no response; gives bitter laugh)

Cat got your tongue, Butcher.

(then)

Bunting was always pissing on about cats, wasn't he? Now he's bombing out in true Alice in Wonderland style. Name of that cat? You don't know, Butcher. I don't know, but you don't *really* know, right? Listen to me, man. Who bothers to talk when we're alive?, and then we get... nearly not alive... yeah, nearly not alive, Butcher, and all we want to do is talk, talk.

BUTCHER (fiercely) I'm not going to die like this, Cass.

CASS (monotone) Good.

BUTCHER There was an explosion first. You hear it?

CASS Roll on, roll on.

BUTCHER Don't go getting like Bunting on a man, Cass. You hear it, I asked.

CASS Yeah.

BUTCHER So it must have been a blower. They must have let the gas build up. The stupid dumb bastards!

(He smashes the palm of his hand into the rock, then tries to 'melt' into it)

CASS Cool, Butcher. Stay still.

BUTCHER Don't keep talking to me like that, Cass. You ain't my bloody old man.

CASS Alright.

BUTCHER Cass… I'll take most of it, but this isn't right. This is…

(He is starting to make himself sick)

CASS Say it, my friend.

BUTCHER (near choking) … fucking horrible.

CASS Yes.

BUTCHER *Horrible*, Cass.

CASS Yes. Say it, Butcher. Get it off your chest. You gonna alter it by saying it? Because you might, Butcher. Try, homo sapiens. God in your fingertips, snap snap. You're a magician come down the human line, Butcher; you're got the magic puff of smoke at the end of the millions of years of us clawing up. So, go on, God's choice, pull the caper out of the stinking rabbit hole.
(equally as surprising as Bunting's outbursts☺)
BUTCHER, YOU BLOODY LISTEN TO ME!

BUTCHER What's wrong with you?

CASS You ever sat and watched a sunset hummmm at you, Butcher? Like it was melting, oozing at you,,, cornball stuff like that?

BUTCHER We going to just sit here?

26

CASS   For a while.

BUTCHER   I'm asking what're we going to do.

CASS   For a start, mate… we, yeah, we spout wings, right?   We spout scythes.   We spout scything wings, Butcher.   We buzzsaw off.   We disproof Nature.
(makes farting noises)

BUTCHER   I'm coming over to you, Cass.   If I don't feel you, I'm going to be sick.

CASS   It's just shock, Butcher.

(Unexpectedly, he doubles up with pain to his stomach)

BUTCHER   Cass…?

(He starts to go towards Cass, but freezes when the ground begins to shake.   From seemingly everywhere at once, there is a rumble that comes from a fearful depth.   It grows until at its very crescendo Butcher is screaming along with it.   Cass is in too much pain to react.   Bunting, however, seems aroused by it.   He talks his mumbo-jumbo loudly through it)

BUNTING   Oh, yes, found out didn't I how he had smashed the mother cat's head in with a hammer and yes thrown it out with the rubbish.   Did I see.   And then that an put the kitty-kitty down the lavatory alive and I took that madman to court over shooting cats through the back legs.   Crawling along.   Dragging their whatnots.

(A second rockfall crashes in around them.

27

Blackout)

4.

(Finally, a sneeze. Instant better lighting up, although the men are still in pitch black.

Cass sneezes a second time, then a third. The dust is resettling. We see how only BUNTING has remained where he was and unperturbed. Butcher re-emerges almost reluctantly from beneath scoria. When he has recovered enough to grope around again, he manages to find Cass's feet and gets kicked off.

Cass begins to laugh drily.)

BUTCHER   You alright, Cass?

CASS   Call me champ, Butcher.

BUTCHER   You'd be fucking lucky.

CASS   No, Butcher, you're not reading me. Here's the upper crust of his god-sized space ball falling in on little old Cass and all little old Cass wants to do is sneeze in the championship round.

BUTCHER   (craning his head) Listen.

CASS   If I'd sneezed first, you could have blamed me for the whole dumbdown cave-in, Butcher. But sneezing after, I'm playing at a little tin god. You see, Butcher? Give the champeen a bit of a giggle…

BUTCHER   (still hearing something) Quiet.

CASS You've always been without poetry. Here we are. The whole earth come down on us, blind and black like so you can feel it, and Butcher's still working away on Butcher's feeble little hopes. We stuff that, Butcher, old son. The thing of me still wants to sneeze, see, Butcher. Let me tell you about sneezing.

BUTCHER I heard something.

CASS That's not the point. Sneezing...

BUTCHER (feeling it on his face) I've got air!

CASS Sneezing might be thought to be clearing the old snoz...

BUTCHER Cass, air!

CASS (deliberately over him) ... of little irritations.

BUTCHER (hearing something now) Hold it!

CASS (but going on) So a kilometre o rock fall is a minor irritation, comes in that category, see, Butcher.

BUTCHER (with bare belief) TAPPING, CASS!

CASS (singsong) I hear youse knocking but youse can't come in. Just some old bones rattling, Butcher.

BUTCHER You crazy?!

(He find a rock, begins to tap back urgently)

29

CASS (mockery of a shout) Can't come in. Can I come out?

BUTCHER Shut it, you fool!

(and tries to listen to responses to his own tapping. At least in himself, he becomes more and more confident that he is getting responses from above and begins to get more and more confident)

BUTCHER (excitedly) Hear that?

CASS I sneeze hard enough, Butcher, you think I could clear all the passages from here to eternity? See the headlines: 'Cass Sneezes out the Sniffers'.

BUTCHER There. Hear *that*?

CASS I sneezed. I wish a sneeze. Butcher, I sneeze a wish. I am the very champeen of my mind, Butcher. This setback I regard meaningless and temporary and meaninglessness temporariness, Butcher, and…
      (same careless tone)
I think I've been hurt bad, Butcher. Boo hoo.

BUTCHER (unheedingly) We're getting through, Cass! You little fucking bottler!

CASS (audible smirk) Butcher, you will never die.

BUTCHER Start tapping. Get at it, Bunting!

CASS Bunting, he says.

BUTCHER Get at it, Cass!

CASS Tap, tap. Okay? Forget it, man.

BUTCHER (convinced about getting results) Oh Jesus, they're there, Cass!

(But Cass has gone back to lying as still as he can)

BUNTING (somehow understanding, but tapping like a child and setting his rhythm of his words to it) When I went around didn't I the fat Greek was giving away kitty-kitties to the children in his shop. When after did I see them throwing them onto a roof and all those concrete drives below. They lay there.

BUTCHER Shut up shut up shut up!

(Blackout)

5.

(Butcher is still tapping but is now having difficulty keeping it up as his illusions fade. CASS looks as though he is sleeping. But he comes to start to shake violently. Butcher keeps looking venomously in Cass's direction as though the other man has been the cause of the tapping not being successful.)

BUTCHER (not realising Cass incapable) Take over, Cass. God damn you.

(Cass manages to sit up, managing a grin, but his voice is trembling)

31

CASS If He existed, wouldn't you reckon he would have damned me already, Butcher?

BUTCHER They're still answering, Cass. Getting nearer, on the right tack…

CASS Maybe they know the way of the damned.

(Butcher has to drop his rock, rests)

CASS How long have you been doing that?

BUTCHER Yeah, pretend away, matey. Your turn.
  (no reply, finds this one strange)
You've been moaning. You hurt?

CASS Nothing to you. Bunting?

BUTCHER He's still giving me the willys.

CASS His right to one third of the worm hole, Butcher.

BUTCHER Yeah, well…
  (then)
He always was off his rocker a bit. Useless.

CASS (calls) Bunting?
  (but nothing)
Useless, how?

BUTCHER (hotly) Useless as a pisshole without the hole but a bloody side wetter.

CASS I'm useless too, Butcher.

BUTCHER (quietly) I don't know what you're playing at, Cass.
You could be hurt. You might be bludging on a man. I don't
know. What can I see? I'm burning up alive too. I'm bloody
suffocating here, but at least I'm trying.

CASS (claps ironically) You're a wonder of human architecture,
Butcher.

BUTCHER Up yours too, sports star.

(resumes his tapping. Relative silence)

CASS Mind you, you've got the air there, Butcher. Say you
didn't have the air. Air's a funny thing. You try touching it,
Butcher. Better. You try touching without it. Way I figure is we
only rate… Butcher only rates…because of something we can't
touch, Butcher. 'Air.' Say it. Roll it around your tongue. 'Air.'
That's you you're not saying. Why aren't you saying it, Butcher?
Because it sounds bloody stupid, right? Well, that's you that you
not saying, Butcher, because it sounds stupid. You getting frantic
because you can't get enough air or enough you, whatcha reckon?
Same thing, or what? Butcher?

BUTCHER At least I'm tapping, mate.

CASS We suck in air, Butcher, or does air suck us out?

BUTCHER (fiercely) *I'm getting out of here, Cass!*

CASS   The air in here not good enough for you? You not good enough for yourself in here? And useless Bunting, Butcher. And useless *me*.

BUTCHER   Stuff Bunting and stuff you, Cass. Just get over here and keep tapping.

(He can't see that Cass has another spasm of pain and can't stop grunting over it. Butcher stops, listens, lays down rock, crawls towards him)

BUTCHER   Cass?

CASS   Keep away from me.

BUTCHER   What's wrong? What can I do?

CASS   It's… not that I never liked you, Butcher. And it's not that I can't seem to get away from you. It's just that I don't want to die with you. Just don't… come near me. Not much to ask.

(pause. Butcher absorbs this statement. Even he realises how it changes being together in horror to going back to their old animosities. He crawls back to his space)

BUTCHER   Big man.
       (Cass laughs)
I can take you apart with one hand, bugger you.

CASS   But I always got the pats on the back, didn't I, Butcher?

BUNTING   (not knowing how timely the burst is) Frequently. Didn't you see? Frequently in the rubbish bins alive. Barely, I thought. I think. Tied to a brick. Gagging. And the grey tab hanging from the fence tied by the legs. Long time before I got there. I said... I said... didn't I...?

(then clear shout)

Boys?! You there?!

(This startles the other two)

BUTCHER Bunting...?

(But Bunting only resumes his mumbling to himself)

BUTCHER Bloody hell

(then shout in Bunting's direction)

STUPID OLD SHITHEAD!

(then to Cass's hard laugh)

Cass, let's get along in this. I don't mind telling you, I'm packing them.

CASS Of course you are, you goon.

BUTCHER *Jesus, it's so black!*

CASS (monotone) You've got your tapping. You've got your air. You even think you touch, feel, smell both of them. Butcher, you're going to be alright.

BUTCHER Help a man out, Cass.

CASS You know why you're going to make it, Butcher? Because you'd do anything to survive. I mean we all do, but you come right out with it. See, you know what I think, Butcher? I think you haven't got enough imagination not to survive. Tap, tap. Knock on wood.

(But of course, Butcher can't see Cass tapping his head as illustration)

BUTCHER (hardening) Yeah, alright, big sports star. But I'm the one calling them in. Tap tap yourself, smart arse.

CASS Say, Butcher, apart from recently, you ever had a doubt in your whole life? No, really.
(no reply)
Thought not. A doubt's three-parts of an idea, right?, so where you ever going to dreg up a doubt, mate?

BUTCHER You know what I think, Cass. I think you're a gutless wonder.

(Cass starts to laugh at him again but this time it hurts, and then he begins to shake epileptically)

CASS (surprisingly) GOD, NO!

(He scrambles around as best he can looking for what he has lost from his pocket again)

BUTCHER (hiss) You sound like a rat. *Cut it out!*

(Cass manages to take hold of himself reasonably enough, but carries on searching while he talks)

CASS I am a rat, Butcher. I've been scurrying to this for a long time. I've lost something, see. You, you've got your tapping,

Butcher. You've got some sort of cavalry thundering down to Butcher's rescue. You know, if it wasn't around the corner for you, you'd wilt, Butcher. Always the same. Never-change Butcher.

(He gives up the search, lies back tenderly.

Pause)

BUTCHER (quieter) You tell me what else can we do, Cass.

CASS I guess you're doing it.

BUTCHER I'm asking your opinion, Cass.

CASS (now teeth chattering) I guess you're going to sys... systematically search around this tomb, see what you can come up with.

(Pause)

BUTCHER I can't do that thing, Cass. You do it, Cass.
(no helping reply)
I'm not *touching.*
(then)
It's up to you.

CASS Me? I've lost something, Butcher. It's my reason, see.

BUTCHER What's that mean?

CASS You lose reason, you lose the moving part, Butcher. Simple.

BUTCHER I don't dig you, man.

CASS (sloppily tries to sing-song) Don't dig me, Butcher. Dig me out.

(Butcher waits for him to go on, but there is nothing more. He resumes his tapping, then stops to listen, and pulls his head away from the rock face quickly)

BUTCHER Jesus, no…!

(Another rumble grows. This time it advances more quickly. At its height, Cass and Bucher can just be seen screaming through it, and Bunting mumbling manically aloud.)

BUNTING They shaved the cats. Well, didn't they? They lopped the cats from lopping. They wrenched off the cats. They strapped the cats up so they could never lie down. Did I see. Oh, you bet…

(Even his voice is finally swamped out

Blackout)

6

(We hear whimpering as the earth shaking recedes. It is Butcher. Finally the lighting resumes)

CASS Butcher?

BUTCHER (barely) Uh?

CASS Shove that whimpering, Butcher.

(Butcher's reaction to this insult is almost simultaneous. His fright gives way to anger and hatred of Cass, even though the latter is now is constant pain through both injury and obvious withdrawal symptoms and, compared to Butcher, is increasingly finding it hard to hold his nerves)

BUTCHER Who's whimpering, mug?

CASS You were.

BUTCHER I hat your stinking guts, Cass.

CASS That's it.

BUTCHER I'm not kidding, bastard.

CASS Nice of you.

BUTCHER I've always said that one day I was going to do you.

CASS You wanna play toesies for it?

BUTCHER (seemingly the only thing he can think of) You took my woman away from me, *prick*

(This makes Cass laugh openly)

BUTCHER You're a mongrel, Cass.

39

CASS You're a comedian, Butcher.

BUTCHER You smart pisshead.

CASS You're a cunthead, Butcher. You've got shits for brains.

BUTCHER So help me, Cass, I'm gonna see you laying on your back.

CASS You dummy.

BUTCHER You... suckhole.

(Cass lightens the situation with a dry laugh. In the dark all this aggression has been ineffectual but at least it has provided a necessary catharsis to bring them back to the reality of their situation)

CASS Tubes cleared now?

BUTCHER Yeah, well, you still took away the only female I ever wanted, bugger, you.

CASS I'll bite. Who was that?

BUTCHER Carol, and you'd better know it now, Cass.

CASS Carol.

BUTCHER You heard me. Shithead.

CASS Yeah, but which Carol, Butcher? There's been Carols. Oh, Butcher, there's been Carols.

BUTCHER That's right, big shot, play around with it. You married here and you ditched the only woman I ever wanted whether you liked it or not, and I vowed I was going to get you for that one day.

CASS Oh, that Carol. She dropped you like a steaming pile of crud, didn't she?

BUTCHER You've got it coming, mug.

CASS What did you reckon you'd done, Butcher... paid a deposit on her? Put her on lay-by? The idiot box, her, a new three-bedroomer, new vehicle... all one neat bundle of joy, Butcher? You reckon you were capable of that, Butcher.

BUTCHER Better'n you, bastard.

CASS She might have wanted an achiever, mate. Not you. An achiever, see. Me, Butcher. After all, what else are we higher animals here for, or haven't you cottoned on to that in your old age?
    (Butcher growls)
We're here to have to achieve, Butcher. It ain't easy. We're here to think it out, and thinking it out's a real bugbear, believe me. We have to carry the load of thinking before we can go the lay-by escape hatch, son. You can go around looking like a bloody rooster with your latest lay-by thingo on parade but we've got to do the heavy brain stuff lifting. Like now, Butcher, right"

BUTCHER What're you on about,?

CASS Now. Who's gonna think us out of here. It's called the fly in the ointment, Butcher.

BUTCHER Like always, you're farting not yakking.

CASS *More, don't you see, dopey?* Who's going to have to take it on if we don't think our way out of this?

BUTCHER Bugger you, you bugger.

CASS Well, well... *that* Carol. The love of my life as I remember. So what's the beef past the old post, matey?

BUTCHER IT MATTERS NOW!

CASS (stops to think on that, conceding) Maybe. No. No, it doesn't.

BUTCHER (conclusive accusation) You did her down, prick.

CASS (suddenly anguished) *Yes.*

(Blackout)

7.

(This scene played in total darkness without lighting even for audience.

Cass's breathing starts to become stentorious over Butcher's tapping and Bunting's babbling. Cass's voice, too, is noticeably starting to thicken)

BUTCHER Hot. Cass, you stripped?

CASS Yeah, maybe.

BUTCHER I'm burning up here.

CASS I know.

BUNTING (burst) Cats. Didn't I see them in cartons for the rubbish tip dumped! Yes. And scratch, scratch on the cardboard, oh yes! And when I turned that corner that cat had its back leg tied to its head. Running away from me sideways on threes!

BUTCHER (spooked again) CASS?

CASS Still here, Butcher.

BUTCHER Not like this, Cass. I don't want it like this.

CASS Tap. Function. Tap them up even though they don't know it, mate. Get 'em up from the depths of hell.

BUTCHER You could tap with me, Cass.

CASS Shit, you want me to hold your hand?

BUTCHER *A man's not a human being down here!*

8.

(Lighting returns.

43

Butcher and Cass are not stripped as best they can, since it has become so fiercely hot down there. Cass is doubled up. Though his movements are of someone in agony, they also begin to take on a sleepy, surreal quality, previously only indicated occasionally by his voice)

BUTCHER   What's wrong with you?

CASS   Butcher, how much 'soul' you reckon you've got left in your bones?

BUTCHER   Knock it off.

CASS   No, I'm asking. It ought to be important, mate. No sight and all that. 'Souls'... you 'soul'... Butcher, ought to be singing hallelujah and busting to get out. What's the point of carrying one around with you all your life if it doesn't do what it's supposed to when the time comes? 'Come out soul and explain yourself!' Butcher. Butcher. Butcher.

BUTCHER   Shitsake, what?

CASS   You know where my 'soul' is right now? Crabbing around in my skin trying to hide, Butcher. *Cringing.* Crawling around in fear like it never asked to be dumped in this world. Digging its claws in. Mate. Mate.

BUTCHER   Oh, Christ.

CASS   Christ? Yeah, you're right. I'm not saying that Christ didn't have it the worst, Butcher, but at least he had the sky to look up into. At least he had something sorta... noble... to fall back on. At least he had something to melt into. Who'd want to melt into any of this? You're right, soul! Stay where you are!

(impatient pause before:)

When we go where's the rosary, Butcher? No rosary, mate. No shiny little coloured beads. When we flip out, we're gonna go filthy and greasy and grimy and shit all over us and not even our souls wanting to associate with us. *Animals.* They won't come down to get us. They'll decide it'd be too embarrassing if they found us. They'll say to our families: stay with any recent photos. Dirty, butcher.

BUTCHER (new urgency) Cass, I want to tell you something.

(doesn't wait)

I don't know what happened to you, Cass, but I want to tell you something... that I'm not getting any tapping back. I dunno now if I ever did.

(still no reply)

All I saying is...

(but can't spell out any defeat; get angry again)

You talk to me, big sports star. I don't know what's happening, but I'm not getting any tapping back anymore if I ever did.

(waits, listens for Cass, for tapping, for anything)

CASS!

(Blackout)

9.

(Through the intervening blackness...)

BUNTING (light-headedly) Cat did I see dragging a rabbit trap. Gnawing at its back leg on the go. And cat legs putrid in rat traps. And the weight slung around kitty's neck so it couldn't lift up its head. Oh, yes. Didn't even get across the road. No.

BUTCHER SHUT THE FUCK UP!

45

(There are unmistakable sounds of Butcher crawling over to Bunting and shaking the older man violently. It is a murderous rage, finally abates.

Lighting returns. Butcher has fallen away from Bunting and is still panting with frustrated violence.)

CASS Keep off the poor old bugger, Butcher.

BUTCHER You gonna stop me?
     (but then remorse)
Bunting…?

(He now retraces himself to Bunting and traces his face with his hands, purring for quietness)

CASS You're going to try to do us both in, Butcher?

BUNTING (whine justification) There's no tapping anymore, Cass.

CASS Butcher to the end, is it? Might is right, right? How does it go?... the weakest imagination, the strongest hold-on? That you think you can means you're too dumb for words, matey.

(Butcher is stung to crawl back to his 'space'. There he defiantly resumes his tapping, his listening)

BUTCHER They're around, Cass. Small fall. Setback.

CASS Crap.

BUTCHER I'm telling you, Cass.

46

CASS   Crapulence, Butcher.

BUTCHER Help me tap, you prick!

CASS   Mate, can't you see I'm trying to get it over with, not drag the laugh-on-us out. You're a goon, Butcher.

(Pause)

BUTCHER (fearful whisper) How many you reckon?

CASS This section at least.

BUTCHER   No, how many in all?

CASS   This section, has to be at least a hundred. Both shafts? How can guess?

BUTCHER   Jesus.

CASS   Does it help to know how many of us, or not know, Butcher? Because one way or another it should help. Answer?

BUTCHER I'm coming over to you, Cass.

CASS   No, you don't.

BUTCHER Put out your hand. Tap or something.

CASS (relapsing) Go and get… tapped yourself.

BUTCHER   That last fall get you, Cass?

（no response）

Hey!

CASS (coming back) Aw, wise up, man. I got hurt. I think I'm even bleeding pretty badly. In there. In. Feeling bruised. So what's that, Butcher? I've lost 'em. I've lost my life's balls. Trying not to go berserker, see.

BUTCHER (stopped) You were supposed to be cured.

CASS They call it drying out, Butcher. If I'm bleeding how am I dried out? Cured. I am ham. That make you Shem and our daddy Noah? We gonna float on out of here, Butcher?

BUTCHER (something to be contemptuous about) Weak as piss, you, and a liar.

CASS You tap, Butcher. But watch out. Withdrawal symptoms, mate. *I might withdraw*. Poof!, outa here in a puff of smoke. Oh, yeah, I'm going to suffer... lost it, can't find it. Rock Squashes Ice. I...

（suffers pain）

Uh... *Butcher*?

（recovers）

Like that, Butcher. Icy old me. Ice gives you the shits shivering. Butcher, I can hear you tut-tutting from here. You've always been an old hen, Butcher. What're you at church, deacon?

（now having to fight pain again）

Don't you... worry about me, son. This hooked-up friggin' *front thing* that spitzes around the world as me... you oughta see how you know it's rotting every fucking day, Butcher. Rot, rot. You.. you tell me how this down here... in here... how it's much different. Lumps. Lumps bumming out, like a sack of potatoes, son. Lumpy and soft squashy. Your type, Butcher, you'd call it the life that lives. My kind calls it the botfly process. My kind... we're legion, Butcher.

(depressed, Butcher stops tapping)

What's wrong, pal? Tap turned off?

BUTCHER (monotone) They're there.

CASS Cock, and you know it.

BUTCHER You've got a head full of meat, Cass.

CASS No, no. I get it. I do. They've got to be up there for the Butchers of the world, right? I know what goes through that tiny little brain pan of yours, mate... mirages. No imagination, they have to be mirages. All's trudging across the endless plain, right?

BUTCHER You'll get yours, big sports man.

CASS (taking threat seriously) Butcher, it might be the Butchers before any other shithead, but don't get any ideas, pal. I might be going to suffer but I've...

(passing pain makes him take different tack, laughs)

Hey, I was going to say I've got my beadies on you. Laugh, Butcher.

BUTCHER I ain't laughing.

CASS What worries me. Especially when you realise we're not getting any more air in here anymore...

(Butcher reacts. He gropes for a place he has known air's been getting through to find Cass is right. The last rock fall...)

CASS Now will you believe me about the tapping?

BUTCHER They're up there!

CASS Sure they are, and you stick with that. Me, I just sort of figured it was some other poor bugger close by and after that last fall, Butcher, he ain't tapping so well anymore.

BUTCHER Shut your filthy gob.

CASS Watch out for that imagination, Butcher.

BUTCHER Watch out for the eebie-jeebies, junkie.

CASS Don't waste the air, son.

BUTCHER FUCK YOU, THEY'RE UP THERE!

(Blackout)

10.

(Through the blackness, almost inevitably, Bunting's rambling rises to domination)

BUNTING (accelerating) Cats! Tacks driven into paws, were there. Hobnailed in pain and roaming with. Cats! Bellies slashed, guts trailing, did I see. Spasms of cats. Where they lay dying bellies going up and down, up and down. Does the pulse go last? Get out. Move away. Flies on cats. Big blowies going the cats.

And cats blown. Half buried before the licks of fire could be licked out, you bet. Didn't I see. And the little tabbies with their teeth pulled out. Pliers. Toy hammers. Tweezers the whiskers. Tweezer the whiskers. Dontcha. Cats dead at a bloke's feet torso tourniquet'd. Poetry in motion. Oh yes and yes cats.

(fades)

BUTCHER Thank buggery. Useless prick. Cass? You still in the land of the living, dopeboy? Cass. Cass. Cass. Even your name has always pissed me off. You know, Cass, it's curious, Cass. You talk about not going out anywhere near me, but the feeling's mutual, junkie. I don't mind too much not cottoning on about the air. But now *you* pointed it out, I'm having a hard time holding myself back from panicking. I could turn into a raving fucking lunatic. Not... in front of you... bloody Cass.

(rocks back and forth, holding himself in)

If you weren't here, Cass, I would. I would let myself go. And you know what? I know it'd be the juiciest, *suckery* feeling I'd ever have in my life. No bull, Cass. Just drop myself over the side and let my nut loose. But as long as I can hold out, I ain't gonna do that. Not in front of the mighty Cass. Not to give the great Cass the satisfaction. And, too, because I know that'd be the end of the line and I don't know about you, but I'm gonna live. So fuck that for a lark and fuck you, Cass.

(Pause. When he knows he isn't going to get a challenge from Cass, he goes back to tapping, until...)

BUTCHER How much air you think we've got? You wouldn't know, you weak piss. Come to think of it, it's just coming home to me how much I've always hated your guts. As long as I can remember... bloody Cass. Cass, the big footie player. Cass, the great headlines man. Champ of champs bloody Cass. And what? All you did finally was flunk out. Smoke it n' dope it Cass. You even run away from your own wife. *My* Carol, bastard. You got

51

had up for dope-arsing y'self and get thrown in the boob, that's all you ever did. Big man Cass. Gonna bring the great wide world down. What'd you ever even finish? I would've given my eye-teeth to have been paid to go to university like that. But you, you crawl back here a deadbeat, a useless fucking *drongo* with his tail between his legs... yet it's still poor Cass. Everybody make room for our shining boy come home. Give the champ his father's job; set him up because he's been injured boo hoo. You've always had it made, bastard, and I've hated you for it. And I'll tell you this, big man.... I'm gonna see you go down first.

CASS (barely) You'd be lucky.

BUTCHER Now I know why I said I'd have you as my side-winder. I've been sweating on the opening to have you, bugger, you.

(pause)

Y'know, my old man spent forty shitty years down here, Cass. Same as my Grandpop. When I was a kid, I'd roll in shit just to smell like my old man then. I'm talking about all *this*. It's always been in my flesh. Now I'm underneath it. You figure that? It's rolling in me.

(madly)

Prickhead, I would've made my Carol happy!

(half controls himself)

And I'll tell you this, mate. Apart from a broken toe, the only thing that got at my Dad finally was the dust, and only then in his ripe old age. And it's gonna be the same for me. And you listen to this, big shot... I never ever wanted to be away from this town. I hate it out there. This is my dust, see, and it's going to take until my ripe old age, too.

(then)

Yeah, you can go all quiet, bugger, you. I hope you're having a hard time of it. I just hope you stay alive until they get here and see the great sports star as he really is. Shit, I can smell you from here. What I think, Cass, is you've shit yourself, like, not even fit

52

company for a man. And I'm gonna be around to tell 'em how the mine didn't get the great Cass but the junkie stuff did. Whimpering. Run away, run away. Bye bye, Mister Number One on the dais.

(snorts)

Superman.

(pause)

God, I'm dry.

(has sudden appalling thought)

God almighty, what if they flood!

(Blackout)

11.

(Lighting returns slowly through:)

BUTCHER Cass?

(is immensely relieved even to get a grunt for a reply)

Must've drifted off. I don't want to drift off. Don't let me drift off again, Cass. I don't want to have to wake up again. I don't want to be near this... this, flying off the handle, most likely. Mate. Cass? Okay? You hear me drifting off like Bunting, you say...

(then)

You had to bring up about the air, didn't you? Bastard, you. I'm no coward, Cass. I'm...

(stops himself thinking along those lines, then:)

Listen, what dya reckon's wrong with Bunting? Why's he gone all quiet? Hey! Bunting!

(He crawls over to the older man, shakes him, but Bunting doesn't stir. He puts his head to his chest, feels the head wound. Nods, then crawls back to his own space)

53

BUTCHER His bleeding's stopped. Dunno what it is with him. At least he's not giving a man the shits. What's wrong with the old goat. You ever hardly heard a word out of him normally, Cass? Like they used to say, you should drop him down the shaft instead of the lift just to clear his throat. Crapping on like that. Cats. Jesus. We end up down here and Bunting turns out to be a fucking loony. How would it be ending up like that?

(remembers another grievance)

Don't give me all that crap about me chasing material things, bugger, you. I mightn't be as pouncy clever-dick as the great Cass, but at least I know what I want. Me, I'm never forgetting the first time I got myself behind the wheel of my first new car, mate. I can still smell the smell of that real leather. Okay, it wasn't real leather. I don't give a stuff. It smelt like real leather. Like my old man used to say, 'Don't feel it, smell it'. I had to scratch and scrimp to get that smell of leather, Cass, and it'll never leave me. I don't care what the great high'n'mighty Cass says that smell was worth every penny. What it did, see, what it did was it made me feel like I belonged. Yes, mug, bloody ads and all the hype. Who cares? If that's the way it goes, that's the way it goes, big sports star.

(stops until further thought)

Where'd you ever belong, shithead? All you could ever do was light up and draw it into your lungs. Even when you come back here with your tail between your arse cheeks, you tell me you ever belonged...

(gets nothing in return)

And get this, big-timer... what I reckon I want most back is that smell of leather. So, okay chasing things... you tell me a better guide for getting through the day-to-day gunk, mate. Big ideas man.

(Suddenly Bunting begins to breathe laboriously. His breathing in and out becomes so rhythmically belaboured that it becomes alarming. He keeps it up, and it becomes

obvious he is doing not so much deliberately but just as blindly-brutal as his rambling outbursts. Butcher lasts out, until:)

BUTCHER KNOCK IT OFF, IDIOT!

(But Bunting doesn't stop, rather seems to increase the annoyance. Butcher loses control. He scrambles over to Bunting and tears at the old man's head as if he would dash it against the rock. He wrenches; he heaves; he pushes and pulls; he pounds until Bunting suddenly falls silent and Butcher can return to his space)

BUTCHER (but still panting with rage) How're we gonna stop him, Cass? I tell you, I can't...
(then)
I'LL KILL YOU, YOU OLD BASTARD!
(and finally)
Cass, you ought to say something to me, Cass. I don't want to be alone like this. Not down... not down *here.*

(He bursts into a bout of frenetic tapping, then stops almost immediately. He sits back, and, in an odd gesture since he cannot see anyway, sits with his face in his hands. His voice is now deeply imploring)

BUTCHER Bunting... don't. I'm asking you, old man. Stop. Stop it, see. You're using up the air, Bunting. Bunting, I know you're sick. I'm sick too, Bunting. I can't help you. I don't want to move around, see... and I admit it, see... and, fuckit, Bunting, you've got to stop.
(and)
Cass, you still there? Cass, you make him stop. Alright? *Alright?*
Cass, see, I don't think I'm going to be able to...

(simply stops)

CASS (painful effort) Hold on.

(Butcher starts to hear his voice, gets a blessed kick of reality from it, comes back sniggering)

BUTCHER   That's my Cass. That's the prickhead. What's the big dramatic act for? Well, you hold on yourself, junkie, cos I want them turning up their noses at the very stink of you. Big man. Useless to man or beast. Okay, somebody's got to go something and that's got to be me. Okay, big shot. Okay...

(He forces himself to explore as much of the pocket they are in as he is able. It is extremely repugnant for him to be doing so and, against all his sense crying out as they are, it is also an extremely brave thing for him to do. In order to keep himself at the task, he keeps attaching Cass:)

BUTCHER   Champion bloody Cass. Perfect man. World-beater. Hot shit. The golden goose's piss. Example for us all. Drag yourself up by the bootstraps like the champ's doing. Lick Cass's boots. That right, champ?...

(By sheer good fortune he locates a helmet in the rubble. Madly he puts it on, tries to lamp. It works. It floods the cavity with precious light.

For a moment, Cass struggles to his elbows to see what it is, then falls back. Clearly he has the shakes which are causing him great pain through his internal injuries.

Even Bunting shows a momentary interest, then goes back to mumbling to himself.

This is a solidly quiet moment of disbelief, and relief.

Then Bunting spoils it by resuming his exaggerated breathing in and out...

Blackout.)

12.

(At its highest, the area is probably less than two metres high, and even this does not extend very far. It seems that the cavity they are in does extend fairly extensively beyond this, although the light from the helmet doesn't allow the blackness out there to be penetrated.

The effects of the helmet light are not all a blessing. Any movement is played grotesquely against the side walls of the rock... frightening in their circumstances, and only serving to accentuate the oily, we nigrescence of the rock.

At least one prop can be seen clearly to have splintered badly, while another, which is taking the main weight of the hanging wall above them, is clearly shaky.

At the beginning the very definition of their situation fills Butcher with fear and loathing. Finally, he adjusts to the new perceptions as much as humanly possible, trapped down there like that. He has got himself able to search around but he finds nothing which could help them.

He can now confront Cass and Bunting. The former, he stands apart from but 'over' and then merely turns away. With Bunting, however, the sight of the older man with his head wound and his oscillating, annoying half-rambling, half-mock-breathing makes Butcher's rage at him even more hard to contain)

BUTCHER You're trying to use up the air, aren't you, you old bastard? Why would that be?

(He gets himself to turn away from Bunting, goes back to Cass, where he can snigger)

BUTCHER Cass, you look disgusting. Take you nowhere, my friend.

(Cass tries to raise himself to what is evidently a threat, but cannot make it. Sadistically, Butcher bends over and presses down on Cass's stomach. Cass cries out in great pain. Immediately, over this,, Bunting's artificial breathing takes on surreal proportions)

BUTCHER (over Cass, hypnotically) Cass. Cass. Cass.

(Blackout.

Then almost immediately, lighting back on. Cass could have blinked. Indeed, for a split second, the cavity is filled with hallucinogenic lighting effects. Then return to 'normal' lighting.

CASS (as though nothing had happened) Here.

BUTCHER (still mesmerically) Cass. Cass.

CASS Here.

BUTCHER (into a hiss) Casssss…

CASS   Whoooo?

BUNTING   (taking up the slow rhythm, but very loud) Breathing for the cats!
(sucks air in and out)
Yes. Doing it, doing it. Suck...
(sucks air in and out)
... suck. Meouw, pussy pussy.
(laughs hysterically)
Breathing for the cats. Did I see.
(sucks in air, lets it out. Theatrically)

(Etcetera.

Cass begins to sway to the rhythm that Bunting is setting. Only after realising this, does he try to break its hold but still struggles unsuccessfully.

The audience now begins to see from Cass's p,o.v. His body is now in wave motion. His entreaties to the 'outside' have the figure of Bunting slowly and waveringly begin to merge into that of Bunting. They seem to melt in with each other at the far end of the area., except that Bunting's tone has become more bullish and mocking, more deliberately malicious. His sucking in and out of the precious air in there takes on an edge of malevolent defiance and of knowing precisely what he is doing.

Cass looks like he is trying to bring them closer and push them away one and the same time, and...i)

CASS   Come in, come in.

BUTCHER   Cass, stop.

CASS Come... *in.* *What?*

BUNTING (starts up madly again) Breathe for the cats.
(sucks in the air madly once more)
I'm doing it. Did I see.

BUTCHER (driven to distraction) Bunt... tinggggg.

CASS Here.

BUNTING Breathe for the. Cats! (gulping the air) Srrrr. Srrrr.

BUTCHER Hunt... innnnggggg.

CASS Come in

BUNTING I'm doing it, yes.

CASS WHAT?!

(Blackout)

13.

(Return of lighting effect from Cass's point of view, but slightly less hallucinogenic.   Pervading all, Bunting breathing becomes less crazy and more as though he is truly having trouble doing so.   For a moment Butcher and Bunting cannot be seen, then they seem to emerge from out of Cass's body.   Again he is trying to hold them in while trying to push them away.   They are mocking him.)

CASS Make streel. Who streel. (chokes back a giggle) Streeled. When cushion cuscus. What's a streel?

BUTCHER Dummy wants to know what's a streel.

BUNTING Meouw, meouw. I'm doing it. Yes.

CASS (enjoying the playacting) A streel, Butcher, is a rrrrr of steel.
(changes tack)
Yes, come in, come down. Shitheads...

(fade to blackout)

14.

(Butcher and Bunting are feeding from Cass who is now in a position of a sow feeding its young. Colours play across them and have a peaceful effect, one of contentment. Cass's arms are flung out widely in a come-one-come-all gesture.

At first Cass is comforted but this soon changes. He starts to honk like a pig, initially softly. But then Butcher's piglet noises become more aggressive, more brutishly going at the teat. Cass's noise rises in alarm. Bunting's kitty-kitty meouwing follows Butcher in aggressiveness intent.

The lighting effect flickers even more cyclically until a peak is reached, when Cass doubles up and tries to get away from the other two, tries to escape from them, but is held back from doing so.

Blackout)

15.

(Cass sits dead still. Sitting by him in yoga fashion are both Butcher and Bunting.

All is silent.

They seem to loom above him.   The silence becomes agitated,, even deadly.

They remain like this for as long as can be borne. Then each begins, starting from deep down, a moaning which builds up into a sort of cacophonic unison. Butcher's is one of anger and bursting violence. Cass's is one of a rising spasm of pain he cannot hold back. Bunting's is a mixture of sad cat sounds and the infantile.

When they are at full pitch...

blackout and sharp silence)

16.

(Return lighting to laughter just beginning to bubble out of all three. One more Butcher and Bunting are leaning over Cass. He is making initial little flurries to get up but without any obvious impediment. His attempts increase in frequency as their laughter at him increases.

Now Butcher and Bunting are physically restricting him, egging each other on to do so. They seem to be smothering him.

There follows a series of lighting 'cut-outs', even of strobe effect, during which the laughing, now openly menacing, is in crescendo. Cass is even screaming but silently. After each,

Butcher and Bunting take up new positions which express their outrageous intrusions on Cass. Butcher sits on Cass's head; Bunting bites his legs; Butcher kneels on his neck; Bunting bites his hip; Butcher slithers down his torso while Bunting does the same the other way. Butcher twists his arm; Bunting twists his leg; Butcher has his finger in Cass's ear; Bunting is pinching his nose...

... until a last quick cameo showing Cass being held by the arms and legs while he struggles frantically.

There is a frieze on this.

Then Bunting's exaggerated sucking air in and out rises even more malevolently. Cass opens his eyes. Above him, their faces are accentuated by the lighting to be repulsive, reptilean.

Cass lets go with a scream finally.

Blackout)

17.

(Cass is now on his own. Bunting and Butcher have withdrawn and sit in the shadows away from him. When they speak to him, their voices are strangely, as though they were coming through a vacuum.

They talk in monotone. Even when Cass doubles up in pain, he does so with a kind of deliberation and tonelessness that indicates his mind is floating free of the reflexes of his body.)

BUNTING Meouw.

CASS Pain here, Butcher. Where are you, Butcher.

BUTCHER Where's Cass.

CASS Come in.

BUTCHER Cass, there's more than meets the eye.

BUNTING (dry laugh) Here, kitty-kitty.

BUTCHER Doing what, Cass?

CASS What?

BUTCHER Don't do it, Cass.

CASS Must. Save us.

BUTCHER Must you have did done, Cass.

CASS Have to, you know.

BUTCHER More.

CASS No more. I can feel things through here, Butcher.

BUTCHER Any meaning?

CASS Is there a flicker see corner sight like?

BUTCHER Corner site shopped, Cass.

CASS Let me go just because I did.

BUTCHER You did.

CASS Let me go, Butcher.

BUNTING (derangedly) Cat got your tongue?

BUTCHER Bunting, Cass.

CASS (agony but still drily) Bunnttinnnggggg...

BUTCHER What I said, What can Cass see? Bunting bloody breathing like that.

CASS See. Uh. See. A long coming. Edges black. Disgusting.

BUTCHER Bunting breathing it all away.

CASS Yes. Butcher?

BUTCHER Cass? Listen. Bunting. Cass, listen.

CASS (agitated by strangely monotone still) Butcher. Your face. I know it was me. Flesh, where it moved, where you put your mouth on me with those talking maggots. All bloody hhhheavinggggs, Butcher. Maggots, see. Let me go as I did it, now...

BUTCHER Smart arse... any meaning?

CASS (childlike) Let me go.

BUTCHER Nobody said about Bunting.

CASS (breaks the expressionless) BUNNN... TINNGGGG!

(Blackout)

18.

(The lighting is now suddenly flickering in colours and confusingly. It bombards the three of them with each other's silhouette.

And then, seemingly impossibly, the three silhouettes come violently together. The impression is that one of them... certainly either Cass or Butcher has leapt up and launched himself onto the other two. The three silhouettes form a violent struggling mass before quietening in movement, drawing apart again, then merging again, this time slowly.

One thing is definite – one of them is struggling with one of the others, while the third is trying to separate them.

Lighting dims.)

BUNTING (deranged, repeatedly, but going to gurgle) Cat gotcha tongue? Cat gotcha tongue?...

19.

(Bunting's suckings of air comes hard, then suddenly stops altogether. One of the figures moves guiltily away from another. The first figure slides down to the ground. The

third figure remains looking on, not moving. The second figure looks to be suddenly dry retching.

Blackout)

20.

(Butcher's silhouette remains motionless behind Cass, who is now back in his 'normal' position. Cass begins to trace something on the rock above his head, but having done so suddenly tries to knock it away. It is though whatever it is falls to the ground dangerously by him. He cringes, but then seems to notice something else on the rock above, sits up, tries to knock whatever it is away too.

The lighting starts to become more profuse, reminiscent of cockroaches and centipedes scampering on the rock, on himself. The effect begins to invade Cass. His panic now is open. He cries out. The cry is pathetic.

Butcher's silhouette detaches itself from the wall and he comes over to hold Cass down. Butcher slaps him, not without a good deal of pleasure in it.

CASS   (clinging on) Such a dread, Butcher.

(He tries to struggle away from Butcher and, even though his actions are still disabling, he now starts to show that the climacteric is beginning to pass.
Blackout)

21.

(Lighting is even and 'real' again. Cass is still doubled up but is relatively in charge of himself once more. Butcher is

back in his old place and has resumed his tapping, this time with a morose and near hopeless cadence.

The body of Bunting is off to one side... obviously deliberately moved to there.

Once again, there is a growing rumble in the mine. It mounts in intensity and proximity.

Cass noticeably braces himself. Surprisingly, Butcher is able to laugh at him, even as this next rumble threatens to come down upon them.

It passes)

BUTCHER You can tell me now, Cass.
    (gets no reply)
Nothing to say, Cass?
    (still nothing)
You're a real fucked-out case, aren't you, Mister First-past-the-post. Hey, Cass! I'm glad I've seen it.

CASS (without looking up) How long?

BUTCHER You sniveling like a wimp? Who cares?

CASS They'll come again, Butcher. Question. Do I hope there's enough time for them to come again?

BUTCHER There'll be time. I've got the light and they're sure as shit coming, bonghead. You're gone this time, Cass.

CASS Slit open, am I?

BUTCHER   Like a fucking mullet, mate.

CASS (looking about) You wonder where we getting the air from, Butcher?

BUTCHER   What're you on about?

CASS We should be gasping like your mullet by now. We should be in for it. Must be fresh air coming from somewhere.

BUTCHER (excitedly) You're right!

(He casts around again but still can't find any air source)

BUTCHER Doesn't matter where it comes from.

(resumes his tapping. It is then that Cass notices Bunting's body set apart. It is startling)

CASS What's wrong with Bunting?

BUTCHER   Yeah, play the idjit, bugger, you.

CASS What's going on?

(Since Butcher is not forthcoming, Cass raises himself enough to be able to crawl over to Bunting but, before he gets halfway, Butcher throws a rock at him. Cass stops, then starts again. This time Butcher throws a large rock directly at him)

BUTCHER Don't try it, mug.

69

CASS (hiss) You tell me what happened, Butcher.

BUTCHER You tell me, hot shot.

CASS (can now muster up menace) I said, explain.

(Butcher leers at him as though he knows something about Cass now and is keeping it to himself. Then he finally shrugs so-what:)

BUTCHER Old buggerlugs keeled over in my arms. The story I'm sticking to, see. For the time being, Cass... for the time being.

CASS Just keeled over like that.

BUTCHER You know it, pal.

CASS You were going at the poor old sod before I went out.

BUTCHER So what?

CASS And now we've got plenty of air.

BUTCHER Who was to know about that then?

CASS I'm going over to look at him, Butcher.

BUTCHER You've done enough damage, you fucker.
        (pause, then speaking with a blackmailer's equivocation)
He kept sucking our air in and out. No reason except bloody-mindedness. Maybe it was... what d'you uni smart arses say?...

70

extenuating circumstances. Yeah, pull this one. But you're right, who knew about the air still coming in then?

CASS I didn't say...

BUTCHER (over him) I'm not saying one way or the other. Only he gasped then lunged at me. I held him. What can a man do? Then he rallied, like, as though he was seeing me for the first time. You listening, Cass, you prick? You'll laugh at this. He said something about cats down the old mine shaft. With a straight face that was. Then he slipped down me. The least I could do was let him down, Cass.

CASS Is he dead?

BUTCHER Don't come that act.

CASS Dead, Butcher?

BUTCHER Comedian.

CASS So Butcher's making sure he at least's getting out of here, right?

BUTCHER I've got the light, Cass. I got the legs. Flooding holds off and we're gonna be alright. I'm pulling you through to answer a few questions, you weak turd.

CASS Not so weak. Don't tell me, pal.

BUTCHER Who'd want to bother, Big Man.

71

CASS So everything's jake because Butcher says it's jake. All we're supposed to overlook is the small fact that Butcher has…

(stops)

BUTCHER (hiss) Has what?

CASS You know it, Butcher.

BUTCHER You say it.

CASS Don't try anything.

BUTCHER I did Bunting in. That what you're saying?

CASS You said it, Butcher.

BUTCHER YOU DID BUNTING IN, CASS!

CASS (stunned, before…) No..

BJTCHER Tell him you didn't then.

CASS No way.

BUTCHER Tell him a second time.

CASS (frantic on the possibility) No way!

BUTCHER (leering) Make it a lucky third time, bastard.

(Cass goes to spit an answer back but finds he can't do so. Instead, he picks up a rock threateningly)

CASS Not so weak, Butcher.

(Butcher picks up his own rock and they threaten each other

Before this can happen a gob fire spontaneously starts in the rubble, which both men know could lead to another explosion at worst or using up any limitation on the air they might have left.   Quickly, they both cooperate in shifting the rubble, exposing the fire and putting it out.

There is a small moment of incredulity before each picks up his rock again and back off warily from each other.

Blackout)

22.

(When lighting returns, Cass and Butcher have resumed their places but remain with rocks to hand. Occasionally Butcher taps and receives a mocking laugh from Cass, who gets in turn an up-yours finger.

Another rumble comes, but this time they are getting used to hearing them far away. It quickly passes)

CASS Scared, Butcher.

BUTCHER Not of you, sports star.

CASS I'm scared, Butcher, but that's only because I've got an imagination to imagine a no-morrow on the next horizon. Keep up...

(taps head)

the emptiness up here, buddy boy.

BUTCHER I'm keeping you alive, Cass. Take your hand away from that rock.

CASS After you.

(They tense together again until Cass eventually snorts)

CASS Pathetic.

(then)

Like I was saying, Butcher... that no-tomorrow, it's like that light of yours there. It... throws light on things, wouldn't you say? But if that bit of the jigsaw puzzle of no-tomorrow isn't there sudden-like... like your light, Butcher... well, it's not normal, right? Not Butcher's normal. But, you see, you dummy, it *is* normal. It's not-there normal, see. That's what those synapses running around that mush up there of yours can't twig onto, Butcher. And what does that say about you and old Bunting there? It goes you got the wrong victim, mate. That no-tomorrow possibility makes you the real victim of little old Butcher, Butcher. You got the wrong man, you dumb ox.

BUTCHER Speak for yourself, ice-picker. You can spout all the shit you want, but I said you're gone this time, bloody Cass, and I mean it.

(Butcher makes a show of putting his rock down, but Cass doesn't trust him and doesn't follow suit)

BUTCHER   Getting the shits up, is the great Cass?   Afraid of Butcher and so it comes out. About Bunting.. Maybe he was pegging out anyway.   What do I know?   Maybe he was trying to take us with him.   I don't know.   Maybe... nobody'll ask.

CASS   Maybe somebody will ask.

BUTCHER   Maybe.   Maybe not. What I'm trying to do here, Cass, is calling a truce.

CASS   Maybe you are.   Maybe you aren't.

BUTCHER   Bunting... might be he's not worth it.   Just saying maybe, Cass.

CASS   I hear you.

BUTCHER   Funny how Bunting got it so bad, going off his tit like that.   Cats.   Chrissalmighty.   Okay, I'm not saying here and I'm not saying there... but all I'm going on about is maybe they'll look at it as a case of either Bunting or us.

CASS   (craftily)   Could be.

BUTCHER   Yeah. Maybe. I dunno.

(Butcher makes a show of going back to his tapping but he is still watching Cass out of the corner of his eye and Cass is of course aware of it.   Nevertheless, this gives them both a welcome respite)

CASS   You say a few words over him, Butcher?

BUTCHER Come off it.

CASS I can't remember any of those Christian lines. 'The Lord is My Shepherd'... how corny insulting would that be. Anything in the bible about cats, Butcher?

BUTCHER Knock it off.

CASS (but cynically) No, straight up. An antsy bastard like me ought to remember what he's being ungod done down over, right? I ought to be able to say, right Butcher you go to church religiously so you won't know a fucking thing... you don't even *have* to know... but me, now I ought to know what to say about me not having any faith in Big Huey when I'm face-to-face with Big Huey. That's what I reckon, Butcher.

BUTCHER What're you shitting on about now?

CASS Jesus, Butcher, hawk up a gorbie and make it as the most imaginative you're going to be today. Bunting being remembered, Butcher. You going to go out hating my guts and me hating yours. That makes us something at least. We deserve something at least. Same with Bunting, is all I saying. Deserves something. Something that rounds off Bunting. Try a thought, Butcher, other than straining over the shit hole. Both of us try.

(Butcher grudgingly nods. Their 'requiem' for Bunting is callous, yet factual, even perhaps truthful, especially since neither was very close to the older man. They also use it as a thankful diversion)

BUTCHER Bunting, he was always just a poor old bastard, far as I could see. He was always getting it in the neck, even the kids having a go at his hump. But walking on. You'd say that much about him. Never drank or smoked, they say.

CASS No wonder he went silly in the head...

BUTCHER Always talking about nothing. Never heard anything about him and cats. The word goes he never once swore. How can a real man live like that?

CASS Dunno?

BUTCHER Dunno.

CASS (taking it up) Bunting. Bloody old Bunting. They called him Humpy, you're right. Or the Hunchback of Knotty Pine, or something. Always mumbling away to himself; maybe he was always spruiking on about cats, but nobody knew. Poofie? Who knows? Before she left him, they reckon his wife used to ride his hump to get a bit. No, she died. Maybe left and died, both. With Bunting, who knows. Who's Bunting?

BUTCHER He stank like water never touched him. Long as I can remember, he was always old. If I'm not wrong, once I heard tell he sexed on with a cat, straight up.

CASS (jokishly) Male or female cat?

BUTCHER (ditto) Female. There was nothing queer about Bunting. There was this rumour he used to sometimes sleep down here to save the effort of going up and coming back down again.

CASS Bunting. What a lad.

BUTCHER Yeah.

(Pause)

CASS Anything else?

BUTCHER (bright thought) I was one of the little pricks who used to throw rocks at him. He shouldn't retired years ago. Wouldn't lay down.

CASS Stubborn.

BUTCHER Stubborn.

CASS Sub borned stub born, shouldn't have been sprayed up against the fence and picked up by his mother. Wife gone, rellies all gone, cats gone. Bye bye, Baby Bunting; you've been...
    (throws it out)
... BUTCHERED!

> *(Butcher reacts. They face up to each other again. An open fight to the death is only avoided when Cass has another spasm of pain, has to fight to hold it in)*

BUTCHER (sotto voce) That what you're going to tell 'em, junkie?

CASS What... else?

BUTCHER And you reckon they'll believe you?

CASS Before you, Butcher. The trouble is there's going to be nobody to tell.

BUTCHER They'll get here, and when they do, you've *gone* this time.

CASS (openly in pain again) Nobody, Butcher. Not even a nod out of Godgob Himself. Nix. Nil. The big fat zero. See, Butcher... whatever might have happened, no Lazarus type revenge for Bunting. All it'll be is if you're still living you grazed better than Bunting, full stop, end of...

(doubling up)

So who's... going to tell Bunting that? You... or... me?

(Is overwhelmed momentarily. Butcher sees his chance and comes on with his rock but he has hesitated too long and Cass is able to pick his own rock up and fling it at the helmet. It's a good enough hit to smash the light.

Blackout.

23.

(In the intervening darkness, clear signs of the two men fighting grotesquely without being able to see each other. This is frighteningly claustrophobic, punctuated by their catching breaths and grunts as they grope around, lunging)

24.

(Lighting for the audience, as previously. Cass and Butcher are performing a danse macabre... groping, moving cautiously, stopping to listen, swinging their rocks about themselves. All they know is the other man is dangerously close by; it is a horror for both... the guesses, the wrong ways, the wild swings, touching and the repugnance of the blackness more overwhelming than the need to come out best.

Cass might be hurting but the impenetrable blackness evens up the situation.

Then comes the next rumble. This is much stronger than the earlier ones and the resulting rock fall more approximate. Their duel becomes comparatively minor. Their fear is reflected in how both literally try to burrow themselves out of harm's way when the tremor reaches its climax.

Blackout)

25.

(The tremor passes)

CASS DAMN YOU, SHITHEAD!

BUTCHER DIE, PRICK!

(Pause)

BUTCHER You didn't have to do that to the old guy.

CASS I'm too had it to tangle with you anymore, pal.

BUTCHER You smashed the light. It was my light.
  (then)
YOU THINK YOU'RE GOD HIMSELF?

(They are lying back from each other. The danger from the other has momentarily passed, but they keep their rocks close to hand and they remain wary of any sudden sound of movement.

Butcher has been really set back having lost his light. It makes Cass now more aggressive, and knowing it)

CASS Butcher, I am a voice. Holus bolus, all that's left of me. I am floating, Butcher. I am around you everywhere. I am *the rock*.

BUTCHER I'll see you in hell.

(He goes back to tapping but is hampered in listening for any reply and listening for any attack from Cass)

CASS So my Carol was your One'n'only, eh? You should've told me. I would've pissed myself laughing. Hey, I could have told her and she could have blamed getting knocked up on you. You didn't knock up my wife, did you, Butcher. Sneaky, creeping in between her legs. No, I don't reckon. You always did plough in behind me, didn't you, loser?

BUTCHER It near killed her when she lost that baby, but what'd you care. This time I win, Cass.

CASS Ah, the razor-blade race for life now, is it? You won't win. You could never win anything.

BUTCHER Big junkhead world beater.

CASS (not unremorsefully) I didn't know why I left her that time, Butcher, and that's a fact. I don't even know if there was any reason or not now. Someone I forget just came along and I guess I thought that's where life went for me. I don't mean your type of 'living', dumbo, not your charge accounts and the back-seat leather smell of your new bombs... Butcher's goodies, right?... I don't mean that. I mean the I-can-have. Something about potential, like all those hundreds of thousands of coaches kept spouting about. I should have listened more. I admit that. But that's not the point.
(listens)

Keep tapping, Butcher, so I know where you are.

BUTCHER I'll tap your head, big shot.

(pause)

BUTCHER She never came back home again. I was waiting for her, Cass.

CASS Not the point, mate. Point is, I got the notion to flow on and she was left standing and I was sorry. I guess I was sorry. I'm not sorry now, is the point.

BUTCHER Suck on this, Cass.

CASS (calmly) Would you really kill me too, Butcher?

BUTCHER I could ask you the same, bastard.

CASS Listen, Butcher.

BUTCHER What?

CASS Wouldn't it be beautiful just to be able to lie back right now and go blank?

BUTCHER (thinks, before:) Yeah.

(Another fire from spontaneous combustion breaks out.

Butcher, more able, gets to it first. He scrambles to get the rubble aside so he can put it out, when he realises he is now

clearly seen against the flame, whereas Cass   *remains*
in the shadows unseen. Butcher scrambles to get away from
the light)

CASS *Put it out, fool!*

(Butcher scrambles back and covers the fire. As soon as he
does so, he gets hurriedly back to his place, resumes tapping
with an urgency brought on by shock)

CASS You check to see if there was any, Butcher?

BUTCHER What now?

CASS Wood lying about. Wood could've made a torch.

BUTCHER Shit!

CASS (real put down) Don't be so thick, Butcher. Never change,
will you?
    (then)
You should've seen your face when you realized you were a
sitting duck against that fire.

BUTCHER They're up there and they're gonna see you get yours,
Cass.

CASS You don't sound too sure anymore, Butcher.

BUTCHER I want them to see what you really are, Cass.

CASS You know, Butcher, I'll go Gladly. Jesus, let it come.
Chrissakes!

> (gets a hold of himself)

Okay. But not by a self-starting fire, mate. Or smoke. Or gas. Monoxide, okay, but not by a blower. Not by a seam of coal, Butcher. Not burning or choking a man off and not...

BUTCHER (outcry) LET THE BASTARD FALL!

(Pause)

CASS Frachet.

BUTCHER What?

CASS Frachet, mate. Like in frachetty. Or ratshit. Okay, you go, you go and there's that...

> (spasm of pain)

Logic. 'Kay. Burning or choking. The longest linger, but what I mean is that's not going out. That's *dying* before you going out. I hate that! That's being killed not being allowed to pass on. But to die... clawing at yourself, Butcher...

BUTCHER Oh, God, man.

CASS Keep tapping, son.

BUTCHER Get knotted.

CASS Wouldn't mind getting knotted one last time, mate.

BUTCHER (thankful for release) Not half.

CASS (ditto) You take the top half; I'll take the bottom half.

84

(sing song)
'I'll be in scrotum afore ye…'

(But any camaraderie ends there at this time. Each goes back to his thoughts)

CASS (only starting off slowly) Son, you go in and come out of that church of yours smiling, so what's with being made in your Big Huey's image when there's more dying than being dead? No, I mean it. What goes with the suffering for years… the pain and the humiliations, like… before you can get to peg out? That thing up on the Cross, that supposed to be a shining example to us all? That was fucking awful, Butcher. That was agony itself, like this is what all you guys'n'gals can ever expect. Where's the nice-and-softly time and then breathing a sigh bye-bye, fullstop?

BUTCHER Don't go even more whacko on a man, Cass.

CASS No, I want to know… that the Grand Design you go for? Jesus wept. Why not a big light switch in the sky and one flick and lights-out; you're outa here no sweat, sayonara? Nothing in between life and death, Butcher. No qualifying event called *dying*. What's this *dying*, Butcher. That Huey's Grand Plan? *Suffer* the little chil'run the only thing He ever no-bulled about? That's just treating us like animals, son. Maybe animals are what we are to your Huey, Butcher. They say animals don't know what's going on, so that's what it looks like to me… being treated like animals. Not human, Butcher. Negative on the dignity befitting one of your ribs. Animals. That the message you've been getting all along from your church but you haven't twigged it, because you haven't lamped onto the animal hooves beneath the robes? Butcher, give me a big light switch in the sky any day. One flick and you're gone.

BUTCHER Yeah, with you, some hope.

85

CASS (near outright panic) I don't want to go out choking on smoke. I don't want to be struggling under water to breathe. I don't want to be screaming in pain under a shit load of rock. I don't want to be gasping towards my last breath a half an hour away. Fuck this *dying* caper. Who said we had to go out *dying* anyway?

(letting go)

Butcher, listen, Butcher…!

BUTCHER I'm listening, mad man.

CASS I'll go, I'll go but… *this ain't right, Butcher!*

BUTCHER Hey, it's bad enough for me too.

(another quietening, gathering moment)

CASS You know, Butcher. A little high here or there made it come back easy enough… even going through the lock-up now'n'again… but coming back here… like, back down here to my old Dad's tunnels… it's where I think I've been coming all my life.

BUTCHER So what? Half of us.

CASS No, what I'm sprigging on about is maybe this's the only thing I've really understood all my born days, Butcher. Here. Now.

BUTCHER Yeah, and I'll say again… so w…

(stops up short, stunned)

I hear them!

(confirms)

I can bloody hear them!

CASS YES!

> *(They both exult and then frantically go at the knocking on the rock faces, now careless of any danger from the other man.*
>
> *But almost simultaneously they come back to their reality that they would be murderous to each other and also the problem they have with Bunting's death.*
>
> *They move apart again, face up to each other)*

BUTCHER Don't get any ideas, Cass.

CASS Speak for yourself, idiot.

> *(Of the two, Butcher is the more confident now. Despite the danger he feels from Cass, he is positively exuberant and goes back to his tapping with gusto as a show of superiority.*
>
> *Cass, on the other hand, quickly seems down and uncaring. He is drifting off in fits and starts again, even starting to shake again)*

BUTCHER   (to up above) Yeah, come on, you big beautiful bastards.

CASS Who cares, Butcher?

BUTCHER You care, big achiever, you care.

CASS I'm hurt, Butcher.

BUTCHER Keep going on about it, and I might believe you, junkie.

CASS You mightn't have any trouble getting over your bullshit about Bunting and me after all, Butcher.

BUTCHER You bet your booties, pal.

CASS (warning) Don't try anything, Butcher.

(Bunting resumes his tapping again, still hearing the rescuers. His exhilaration makes him so full of feeling he has to stop and spout what for him is a long introspection)

BUTCHER You know what I know now, Cass? I've beaten you, mug. This time it's my turn. Always bloody Cass out ahead of me, but not now. I gave ten times the guts you gave, bloody Cass. I stuck it out. I stayed around and slugged it out, because I never had it easy like bloody shining-light fucking Cass. Prick! When you weren't pussyfooting around here getting all the glory, I stuck and I won. I was the top operator around here and don't you forget it.
      (to Cass's reaction to that)
You can snigger, shithead. Big champ. World beater. You wouldn't know what real *sticking* meant. Me, I had to sweat my tit off all the way. Then you come back.. A fucking junkie, a jailbird, a total bloody failure. A deadbeat. And they reckon the sun still shines out of your arse like I was nothing! But, yeah, just so you remember it, I'll say it again, flunk-off... I've beaten you this time.

CASS A fact?

88

BUTCHER A fact, bastard. And they're coming and gonna see what you did and how Cass ain't fit enough to lick my boots, mug.

CASS (softly) I never said I was, Butcher. I just said you're as meaningless as me.

BUTCHER (after stopping to think on that) I almost feel sorry for you, Cass.

CASS I feel sorry for you, Butcher.

BUTCHER I mean that, Cass.

CASS Butcher, so do I.

(They pause to peer hard in each other's direction. It is as though they are re-assessing the other man. When Butcher goes on, it is markedly more conciliatory...)

BUTCHER What'll be going on up there? The alarm. That. Did you ever hear it? I did once. My Mum froze on the spot. Her face went white. All night standing around. Waiting. Dead still. The cold white breaths. The TV and all the outsiders. Sure. Hey, Cass, we'll be on Nine's news for sure.

(stops on thought)

Who'll they show up there waiting? For Bunting, not a red fig. For you, Cass, who?

(Cass doesn't answer because they'd be no one either)

Big man, bit zero. For me? All me mates, my mob, me back-up?

CASS Maybe for ten minutes and then into the pub.

BUTCHER (quiet acquiescence) Yeah.

89

CASS   You know something Butcher?

BUTCHER   Yeah?

CASS   You can come and get me now, melonhead. What do you want me to do? Bleep while you home in?

   (Butcher contemplates that only for a moment before he throws his rock away)

BUTCHER   Take it easy.

CASS   Come on then.

BUTCHER   Up yours.

(They lean back.   This is a precious moment of relaxation.

   Then Butcher resumes his tapping and listening. But he pulls up abruptly. Taps harder, listens more intensely. Then…)

BUTCHER   (disbelief) I think they're gone again, Cass.
   (frantically taps)
They're not answering. Cass?
   (then)
WHY?!

26.

(Through the darkness we hear Butcher madly backing his rock against the rock face. He has to give up momentarily through exhaustion of having little air

The 'audience' lighting returns)

CASS Steady, son.

BUTCHER No, mate, no…

CASS You've got it.

BUTCHER I keep telling you don't talk to me like a fucking child, shithead.

CASS That's it, Butcher.

BUTCHER What's fucking it?

CASS See, how it all comes back to the beginning? Butcher?

BUTCHER Up yours with the butter knife.

(Now they hear why the return-tapping has ceased)

BUTCHER (surprisingly tonelessly) You hear that?

CASS I hear it.

(A very deep rumble then tremor from seemingly the bowels of the earth. There is no doubt about the finality of it. It is frightening oncoming wave rises to full pitch as a background to:)

BUTCHER Cass.

91

CASS Butcher.

BUTCHER CHRIST!

CASS CHRIST!

BUTCHER Where are you, Cass?

CASS Over here.

> (*They grope for each other, touch, stay besides one another.*
>
> *They are now starting to get thrown around.*
>
> *Cass moves particularly)*

BUTCHER *What are you doing?*

CASS Waving my dick, Butcher.

BUTCHER What?

CASS Waving my dick.

> *(pause before:)*

BUTCHER Ain't much of a dick, Cass.

CASS Still beats yours by a mile.

BUTCHER You wish, mate.

CASS Any rate, what're you doing, Butcher?

BUTCHER I'm waving; what else? A bloody flag, Cass!

CASS Butcher, this dick here almost had it good…

BUTCHER You're not kidding!

(They keep shouting defiance to encourage each other before they are drowned out. Their mouths are still moving when

the final cave-in comes)

###